THERE'S MORE TO MUSICALS THAN MUSIC

Compiled by
Grace Hawthorne

Chapters by

Martha Eddins
Gilda Gant
Howard C. Parker
Martha Rush
John F. Wilson

SOMERSET PRESS
Carol Stream, Illinois 60187

FOREWORD

In the past several years I have had a chance to hear some fantastic music performed in churches, schools and community halls. The kids were eager, the audience receptive, the music polished and professional.

This book is compiled to help you produce musicals that look as professional as they sound, without hiring additional staff members, going back to school for a dramatic arts degree or losing your sanity.

I have worked with all of the writers of this book and I'm excited that these professionals have agreed to share their knowledge with you. You'll find chapters on staging, sets, costumes, acting, lighting and sound. You'll learn some tricks of the trade that will help you turn your musical concert into a musical production. It can be done . . . with a little help from the friends you'll meet here and your own imagination.

Break a leg!*

Grace Hawthorne

*"Good luck" in theatre parlance

GRACE HAWTHORNE

4

Grace Hawthorne was the catalyst for this handbook. As the creator of a long line of successful musicals, she is constantly being asked for a "how to" set of guidelines in a variety of areas. As a result, she contacted several of her professional friends, each experts in their chosen field. Grace challenged them to put together a simplified guide that could help anyone turn a musical program into a musical production. We think you will agree with us that they have admirably succeeded.

Ms. Hawthorne was born in Salem, New Jersey, and raised in Baton Rouge, Louisiana. She received her BA in Journalism from LSU and published her first musical, LIGHTSHINE, in 1972. This was quickly followed by IT'S COOL IN THE FURNACE, REVOLUTIONARY IDEAS, THE ELECTRIC SUNSHINE MAN, THE SMALL ONE and ENTERTAINMENT-NOW AND THEN, to name a few of her major works.

A dynamic and creative innovator, her accomplishments also extend into the area of educational publication, recording and TV. The author of a patriotic musical by Holt Rinehart and Winston as a part of their EXPLORING MUSIC series, she also served as Associate Producer of a children's album featuring Clifton Fadiman for Open Court Publishers. For a time, Grace was also employed as a lyric writer for TV's Sesame Street and is, in fact, the recorded voice of Belle Matthews on Somerset's new album, ENTERTAINMENT-NOW AND THEN.

The Publishers

Let me introduce Martha Rush. Martha is the Public Relations Specialist for the Georgia Council of the Arts and Humanities. She is also a free-lance actress doing film and commercial work. She trained at the National Theatre Institute in Waterford, Connecticut, and has worked with such well-known companies as the National Theatre of the Deaf, The Looking Glass Theatre (a children's theatre) and the Academy Theatre in Atlanta, Georgia.

1.

CASTING YOUR SHOW

Casting a show can be easy if you follow a few simple guidelines. 1) Choose a casting committee. 2) Determine exactly how many people will be in the cast. Divide them into groups: children, adults, males, females. Then determine the age range you will require. 3) Write an advertisement: State the name of the show you are casting, how many people you are looking for, their age range and their gender. Next state the time and place of your casting session. 4) Place your advertisement on your church or choir bulletin board at least two weeks in advance. 5) If you are doing a church-wide production, have your minister include information on your casting session during church announcements, or advertise in school or community paper. 6) Spread the word. Word of mouth is one of the best ways to notify people about your casting session.

THE CASTING SESSION

The location of the session is important. It is best to hold a casting session in a medium sized room as large rooms tend to be intimidating. Of course if you are doing vocal auditions, you'll need a piano. It is best to have an adjoining room or hallway where people can relax and wait their turn.

The most important factor is to make the person you are auditioning feel comfortable. Everyone comes with a case of nerves and you must do your best to make him or her relax. It is helpful at the beginning of an audition to make small talk unrelated to casting, then slowly work into the audition.

For singing auditions, I strongly suggest having on hand some simple songs people are familiar with and ask them to sing one or two bars off the top of their head. This will give you enough idea about their vocal range and qualities.

Always know what you want, not only age and gender, but what qualities you feel are necessary for the characters you are casting, and be sure your casting committee knows your requirements. Are you looking for a gruff king, a meek boy or a crazy queen? Cast people who possess the qualities you are looking for or who can find these qualities in themselves and portray them.

With a casting committee you will need a standard rating system. I suggest a score card, one for each committee member to be filled out for each person auditioning. Determine how many you will need before hand so you won't run out. Here is a sample card.

NAME _____

ROLE AUDITIONING FOR _____

	1	2	3	4	5	6	7	8	9	10
General appearance						X				
Posture, stance									X	
Movement			X							
Voice projection						X				
Diction		X								
Stage presence						X				
Concentration	X									
Direction									X	

Comments:

Look for the quality of concentration. Can the person remain involved with the action of the play and not break concentration?

Can he understand and follow direction from you? Tell each individual how long it will be before you make your final decisions.

This is where the score cards will be invaluable. Meet with your committee as soon as possible after the auditions and tally the scores. Once you've narrowed the field, you can discuss people and roles in detail. If you are undecided, announce a callback for the people you wish to see again.

As soon as you have decided on your cast, contact each person separately and tell them when and where the first rehearsal will be held.

2.

THE REHEARSAL SCHEDULE

Your rehearsal schedule should be as carefully planned as your casting session. A good framework to follow is an eight week period with either two or three rehearsals per week. This way you can count on at least 16 to 24 rehearsals before the opening of the play.

Naturally you will have to construct your schedule around the needs of your cast, but it is wise to make a definite schedule upon the first meeting of the entire cast. For example, "We will meet every Tuesday and Thursday at 7:30 p.m." You may wish to divide your rehearsal schedule into segments. For example, if you have a group of children who are in the first scene and are not in any more of the show till the last scene, it isn't necessary for them to be at every rehearsal.

Be sure to keep yourself as flexible as possible yet have a structure. Also remember the novelty of rehearsals will wear off as you start into the second month and the real work begins. Remind parents and cast members that to achieve something of value there is hard work involved and that the final product will far exceed their expectations.

The first four rehearsals should be spent with "books in hand" (carrying scripts). By the third rehearsal you should tell the cast when you expect them to have their lines learned. The cast should "put books down" (stop using scripts) by the sixth or seventh rehearsal. Even if lines are not well memorized, it is important to have your cast begin to become comfortable without their scripts. Have a helper sit on the sidelines and prompt the actors if they need help. The remaining rehearsals should be spent refining the play. "Notes," your comments on performances, should be given after each rehearsal. Be sure to give compliments as well as direction. Actors should keep all notes (blocking, interpretations, etc.) in their own notebooks.

SPECIAL REHEARSALS

A few days before the opening of the play, you will need to schedule a "run-through" (doing the entire action of the play without stopping). You will also need to schedule a "technical rehearsal" (a rehearsal using all the effects, lighting, sound and music). This rehearsal will have numerous stops and starts but actors must be on hand to run the action for the technicians. The technicians will need to get a good idea of what comes where and the actors will need to feel comfortable with any special effects. The day before the opening, schedule a dress rehearsal. This is a combination of everything: lights, effects, costumes. It should be run with no breaks, just as it would be on opening night. Tell the actors to arrive one hour before the time set for the rehearsal. This is to allow time for them to get into costumes and makeup.

Give notes to the cast after the rehearsal. Then send them home with plenty of time to rest before THE BIG OPENING. At the end of dress rehearsal . . . no matter how it goes . . . be full of encouragement. Thank the cast for all their hard work and tell them how excited you are about their opening.

3.

ACTING IN A MUSICAL PRODUCTION

Acting in a musical production should be viewed as the base or foundation for the production. Even though the music sounds wonderful, the costumes look beautiful and the scenery is just right, if the characters do not have a good sense of their roles,the production will not have the impact you are striving for.

HOW TO BEGIN

First of all, as the director, you will want to help each actor create and understand his role. Here are some ways to do that.

Meet with the cast and instruct everyone to bring a notebook and his script. Have each actor read through the script three times. On the first reading they are to become acquainted with the story and the characters involved. On the second reading they are to pay specific attention to their character's physical makeup, profession, social class, family background, economic status and, even more important, to his basic likes, dislikes, attitudes, general emotional makeup and ways of dealing with a crisis. During the third reading, instruct your actors to "see" their characters in terms of mannerisms, voice, gestures, stance, walk, etc. Have them start using their notebooks right away to jot down characterizations.

Another way of helping your actors develop their roles is to define what each character wants, what he is trying to do and what he wants to accomplish.

Try this simple exercise. Have each actor write at least five statements about his or her character which have not been given in the character description in the script. Begin with the statement "I want......" For example, the actor playing the part of one of the wise men might write:

I want to see this child.
I want to deliver this gift.
I want to sleep after this long journey.
I want to know what all this commotion is about.
I want to leave because I'm afraid of the Roman soldiers.

All this information should go into the actor's notebook, along with blocking directions and any other notes that you give during the course of the rehearsals.

ACTING SKILLS

Concentration. Concentration means giving a situation your closed or fixed attention. Apply this in directing your cast. Point out to them that memorizing lines and knowing where to stand on stage is not acting. Actors must block out everything other than the action on stage. They must be totally involved in the story at all times, i.e., they must stay in character. As a director you can help inexperienced actors by suggesting reactions to them and making sure that everyone on stage feels a part of the action.

Relaxation. This is an important factor in concentration. Before each rehearsal have your cast perform some kind of exercise that tenses and relaxes the muscles. If you are working with children, this is especially important. Lead them in 15 minutes of supervised exercise before rehearsals. This gets rid of some of their nervous energy and results in a quieter rehearsal.

Body Economy. The body and the voice are the actors' tools. Body economy means controlling expression and movement. For example, a character may be called on to act happy. There are a number of ways you might direct this. You might have him jump up and down, or laugh loudly, or hug and kiss everyone in the room.

Consider this suggestion, "His eyes brighten, a smile creeps across his face, he appears to want to jump up and down, but he doesn't." With that direction, you are teaching your actors to practice body economy.

An audience responds quicker to an actor who does not "show and tell" all.

Another side of body economy is helping your actors train their bodies to do exactly what they want them to do. Again you accomplish this with relaxation. Make moves as clear and distinctive as possible. This helps your characters become clear to the audience. Keep reminding your cast that body economy comes with relaxation.

The Voice. Any actor who can breathe can fill a room with his voice. The voice rides on the breath. Have your actors try this exercise. Stand in front of a full length mirror, place a hand (fingers spread) right below the top portion of the chest. Take a deep breath and exhale saying "ha ha ha ha ha ha" until all the breath is gone. Instruct them to keep the intensity of the "ha's" steady and even. They will notice that when the breath is gone, the voice is too.

Now take your actors into a large room. Repeat the exercise, but this time have them aim their voices at the opposite side of the room. Then have each person listen to his own voice. Be aware of where it is placed in terms of a high or low range. Many times placing a voice lower will improve projection.

Articulation and speech. Articulation is the way in which a person shapes words. Once again have your cast stand in front of a mirror. Have them recite a nursery rhyme as clearly and distinctly as possible. Have them repeat the same rhyme, but this time moving the lips and jaw in an exaggerated manner.

Finally, have them say the rhyme in a normal manner and note the difference.

In performance remind everyone to speak clearly and slowly. Even if he is nervous—or especially if he is nervous—the rule is slow down. An actor's main objective is to be heard and understood. Just as you trained your cast to practice body economy, you must train them to practice voice economy as well. For example, the script calls for anger. The immediate reaction is to become loud. However, show your actors that expressing anger through clenched teeth—holding the emotion in—is much more exciting to the audience. Emotional energy in the voice is power under control.

ACTING TOOLS

If you have a tape recorder, record your actors. Have them listen and understand the quality of their voices. Have them learn what their speaking range is, how low or high they can go. Help them experiment and have fun. Encourage them to use their own tape recorders at home.

Another tool is the mirror. Have them stand in front of the mirror to do voice work and facial work. Experiment making faces. Explore with the actors how far they can stretch their faces one direction or another. Have them look sad, happy, angry, surprised, frightened.

One final and very important tool is health. Without good health an actor won't have the stamina he needs to act. Emphasize the need to get eight hours of sleep, eat a balanced diet and exercise. Remind your cast that their bodies and their voices are their best assets. Taking care of these is extremely important.

4.

CREATIVE COSTUMING

Costuming a musical production can be fun if you use imagination and think in terms of color, mood, style, music and shape and not so much in terms of what is the actual time period of the play.

Costumes should serve three functions: 1) they should set the cast apart from the audience, 2) they should relate to the overall mood of the play (serious, fun, elegant, slapstick), 3) they should provide something interesting for the audience to see.

None of these functions requires lots of money; in fact, forced economy can cause ingenuity with objects and materials you might never have imagined could be used in making costumes.

THE COSTUME COMMITTEE

The first step is to select a costume committee and call a meeting with the committee chairman. Study the script and listen to the album if there is one available. Read and listen several times to get the feel of the play. Have the chairman start a notebook and jot down any ideas that come to mind.

The second step is to meet with the set designer. The simpler the sets (discussed in a following chapter) the more important it is for the costume committee and set designer to work closely together. Establish an overall look: bright, subdued, formal, down-home, modern, abstract. The style of the music should be the major factor in determining the look of the musical.

A NOTE ON COLOR

The importance of color needs to be stressed. Color expresses mood and helps interpret the play. Think of the different reactions to a stage filled with red, white and blue costumes and to one filled with tan, gray and black ones. Each has its place, but what a difference! Keep your colors to a minimum. Pick one or two and then work with different shades of those colors. Always keep in mind the picture you are painting for your audience. If you use too many colors, it's hard for the audience to focus.

Color is an excellent way to set principals (main characters) apart from the chorus. Again, the idea is to draw the audience's attention to the main actors.

For example, if the chorus is in prints, put the principals in solid colors, or save one color for the principals. Put the chorus in red and white and the main characters in blue.

If you have a large cast or chorus, it might be wise to decide color schemes in terms of groups. For instance, all the shepherds in white, the soldiers in red and the animals in brown. Remember that all groups must also blend well together.

INDICATED COSTUMES

In most cases, elaborate detail is not essential as long as the costume clearly indicates the identity of the character. Felt tunics worn over leotards or jeans with symbols on the front of the tunics can identify a queen, a shepherd, a money-hungry businessman, an astronaut, a lion, a crusader—anything. Make the symbols removable and the tunics reversible, and you'll have infinite possibilities. And best of all, tunics don't have to be fitted!

S.O.S. COSTUMES

You can tap a great source of costumes by sending out an SOS to the members of your organization for old clothes, hats, curtains, sheets and bedspreads. Try tie-dying sheets as an alternative to the old sheets-and-bathrobes routine.

Hats are a quick and easy way to identify characters, and they are especially useful when one player has to assume several roles. Put several hatracks on stage and they not only hold costumes, but act as stage dressing as well.

If space permits, have an SOS room or area for storing these items. This avoids having to start from scratch for each new production.

17

PAPER COSTUMES

Paper is one of the best materials available and one of the least expensive. Grocery bags, newspapers, boxes and butcher paper all can be turned into costumes with a little tape, some staples or glue, felt pens, poster paint and imagination.

Staple pieces of paper together in the shape of a cleaner's bag with rounded shoulders, neck and armholes. Then you can paint any costume you desire on the front, from white tie and tails to zebra stripes. Check your library for books giving specific designs and patterns.

MASKS

Paper bags, pieces of cardboard attached to dowels and leftover bits of trimming can become elaborate masks. They can turn a happy face into a sad face, identify a king or a pauper.

PERSONALIZED COSTUMES

T-shirts are an ideal costume for the chorus. Try block printing, stenciling or silk screening the name of the show, a symbol, or the name of your group on the shirts. After the show, they're great publicity for future productions.

GENERAL NOTES

If you are sewing costumes, select designs that don't have to be fitted, such as tunics, vests, peasant shirts, wrap-around skirts. Buy durable material, it will be cheaper in the long run. Use hooks and eyes, snaps or safety pins. Zippers are an unnecessary expense. Try to fold and tuck rather than cut where fitting is necessary. That way you can re-use the costumes with a minimum of effort.

A FINAL NOTE

Imaginative costumes can go a long way in helping your cast—especially children—identify with their roles. They are worth the effort. With a little planning costumes can be stored and used for several years. No production is complete without them.

5.

LIGHTING YOUR SHOW

Lighting will probably be the last theatrical equipment you buy. However, there is much to be said for making the investment, or at least renting equipment for special productions.

ADVANTAGES OF LIGHTING

Of all the technical crafts a director can employ to reinforce the work of his actors, good lighting is one of the most versatile. You not only illuminate the stage and the actors, but you focus the audience's attention and create atmosphere.

Good lighting is not static. You should change its focus to suit the varying moods of the play. Flexibility is the key word in choosing lighting equipment. This requires equipment that is not permanently mounted and can be utilized in different ways for different purposes.

THE LIGHTING CREW

Choose your lighting crew early and have them sit in on rehearsals to get the feel of the show. You will need to coordinate sets, costumes and lights. Have the lighting crew set up their script in a looseleaf notebook. Paste the pages of the script on right-hand sides and leave left-hand pages open for lighting cues. Schedule several technical rehearsals so that crew and actors feel comfortable together.

LIGHTING EQUIPMENT

Ellipsoidal spotlights are generally used in front of the proscenium (stage opening) for lighting the downstage and apron areas. They are also used for side lighting or wherever a very controlled beam is needed. Their range is from 30 to 150 feet. They are equipped with shutters that control the size and shape of the light beam.

Fresnel spotlights are a soft edged light with a diffused beam, ideal for use at close range (10 to 20 feet). They are used for lighting acting areas from overhead positions. They can be adjusted from a spot to a flood focus as needed.

Floodlights, as the name implies, are designed for general illumination. Striplights are strips of lights used for general illumination. They are often supplied with red, blue, green and amber gels.

YOUR LIGHTING PLOT

Any attempt to set up a standard plan for lighting is hazardous, because no two plays or playing areas are alike. However, generally the stage area is divided into six areas. (Illustration A and B)

Two spotlights at 45-degree angles are pointed at each area. Each spotlight should be given a separate color, one cool (blue) one warm (red or amber). The spotlights are aimed to fully light the actors' heads. The edges of each area can be softened by throwing the lights partly out of focus.

If you are forced to use existing lighting—and in many cases you will be—here are some suggestions.

Replace white lights with colored lights (or gels) alternating between cool and warm. Try to see that only the stage is lighted and that the house is dark.

Invest in two spotlights as soon as possible and use them. You can create some dramatic effects with this piece of equipment whether you focus it on a revolving mirror ball for an ethereal look, or on a soloist for emphasis.

Remember that lighting has two purposes: 1) to enable the audience to see the actors and the action, and 2) to heighten the audience's emotional reaction; reds for excitement, blues for subtle effects, etc. One last note, always have at least one extra lamp for each piece of equipment. You will be glad you thought of it when a lamp blows out in the middle of a performance.

Illustration A

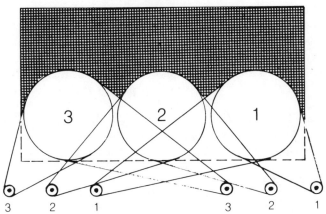

Diagram of lighting plan for downstage acting areas

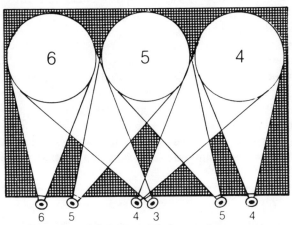

Diagram of lighting plan for upstage areas

Illustration B

6.

MAKEUP

Stage lighting makes everyone look pale. Even if you are not using stage lights, remember that normal makeup looks fine only at relatively close distances. If you want your characters to be seen past the third row, they need stage makeup. This obviously applies to males as well as females.

Basically, stage makeup adds color and contour, otherwise everyone will look flat and pale. Makeup, like costumes, also helps your cast get in character.

If you have a large cast, a choir for instance, makeup helps the chorus feel that they are as much a part of the production as the principals.

Again, the first step is to select someone to be in charge of makeup. This person may want to experiment with special effects, which is fine. The following rules are for basic makeup only.

MATERIALS

You will need to obtain the following materials:

1) A large, strong box with compartments and a lift-out tray to hold all your makeup items. A tool chest or fishing tackle box make excellent makeup kits.

2) Greasepaint in stick or tube form. Also various liners for detailed work.*

3) Liquid makeup for limbs and bodies. Nothing looks worse than a character with a made-up face and a pale body.

4) Blending powders. These are used for blending, aging and setting makeup.

5) Eyebrow pencils in several colors and a small pencil sharpener. Be sure the points are always sharp so that you get clean lines.

6) Cold cream for removal of makeup. If you are working with

---

*You can usually order a basic makeup kit with a selection of items for both males and females from any good costume house. See Suppliers.

teenagers who are concerned about excess oil, it is a good idea to have a bottle of witch hazel on hand to remove the cold cream residue.

GENERAL RULES

1) Apply foundation color and blend over the entire face. Be sure to get up to the hairline, under the nose and under the chin—areas that tend to be missed. Makeup should be applied after characters are in costume. There are two good reasons for this. One, it keeps people from getting makeup all over the costumes as they get dressed and two, it allows those applying makeup to see how much skin needs to be covered. Don't make up a face and leave arms, necks, shoulders or hands gleaming white.

2) Apply color to cheeks from the cheek bone down and out. Blend the edges so as to avoid a hard line.

3) Color eyelids with eyeshadow to match the actor's eye color. Fade the colors at the sides of the eyes. Do not go all the way to the eyebrow. The space between the eyebrow and the top of the eyelid should be the same color as the foundation.

4) Apply color to lips. Red for females, reddish brown for males.

5) Use blending powder that matches the foundation over the entire face. Powder stabilizes the greasepaint before any lines are added. (If you are using lines for age, be sure to use well defined, thin lines, not casual smears. Basic aging can be done by adding crows feet, worry lines in the forehead, and laugh lines from nose to mouth. Graying hair can be done with blending powder.)

6) Apply eye liners. Extend the lines slightly at the outer end to enlarge eyes.

7) Strengthen brows with eye liners.

8) Add a small red dot in the corner of the eye by the tearduct. In females add a red dot behind each nostril.

9) In females apply mascara to upper lashes.

10) Complete the process by powdering again to set all the colors.

If you are doing specialized makeup involving extreme aging, beards, or other dramatic effects, consult your local library for books giving more detailed instructions.

I would like you to get acquainted with Martha Eddins. She is the Director of the Atlanta Children's Civic Theatre which has performed such ambitious musicals as "Oliver," "The Wizard of Oz" and "Tom Sawyer." Martha frequently does summer stock with the Highlands Playhouse in North Carolina. She has been involved with some aspect of theatre for fourteen years. In addition to acting and directing children's theatre, Martha is a free-lance writer and has won several awards for her music and lyrics.

7.

CREATIVE BLOCKING

One thing to be aware of in amateur theatre is the importance of keeping a production visually interesting. Remember your audience sees your musical as well as hears it. Good use of the playing space, variously located stage entrances and exits for the actors, and some element of audience participation can transform a static musical into an exciting production for both cast and audience. Blocking is the physical staging of the players. It can be done in a variety of effective ways. You may use a traditional stage, or a large room, a gym or a recreational hall for theatre-in-the-round (Illustration A) or three-quarter stage (Illustration B).

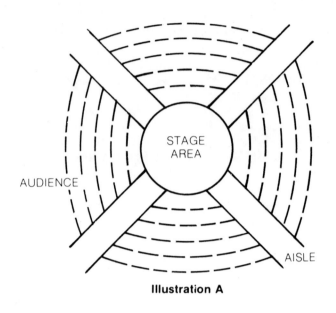

Illustration A

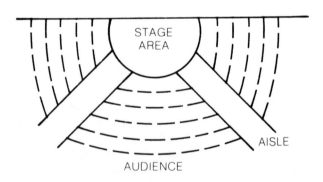

Illustration B

A pulpit area may also be used and we will deal with creative blocking in all of these areas.

BASIC BLOCKING

A few traditional stage terms are important to know when discussing blocking. (Illustration C)

> Stage right—the right side of the stage from the actors' point of view
>
> Stage left—the left side of the stage from the actors' point of view
>
> Downstage—the part of the stage closest to the audience
>
> Upstage—the part of the stage farthest away from the audience
>
> Proscenium—the part of the stage in front of the curtain, sometimes including the curtain and its framework
>
> Centerstage—the center of the stage

```
|-------------------------------------------------|
|                                                 |
|                  UPSTAGE                        |
|                                                 |
|   STAGE          CENTRAL          STAGE         |
|   RIGHT          STAGE            LEFT           |
|                                                 |
|                  DOWNSTAGE                       |
|-------------------------------------------------|
```

Illustration C

Some theatre axioms, such as not turning your back to the audience, are valid. However, keep in mind that the overall picture should look so natural that the audience will not be aware that the action is blocked.

If you are restricted by microphones on stage, try moving people in groups during musical interludes or block only a small number of people (not more than 8 or 10) and leave the majority of the choir stationary.

The most effective blocking uses the whole playing area. For example: a group of children is playing downstage left and another child is to join them. The child should enter upstage or downstage right and run across the stage to the others. In this way the whole stage is used and the movement is visually interesting. (Illustration D)

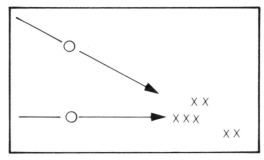

Illustration D

Many blocking patterns come from the scripts themselves. Suppose you have a confrontation between two women. If the women are "catty," the idea of two cats evokes an immediate blocking pattern. Have the women circle each other, watch each other, circle again and then perhaps pounce—physically and/or verbally. Remember to think visually when you read the script and study the music.

As you are blocking, keep in mind the way we speak and move in reality. We do them together. We are a continuous flow of words and movement. We lean on things. We handle things. This naturalness should carry over into your blocking.

Here are some techniques that will help. First, when handing something to someone on stage, or when using a one-handed expansive gesture, instruct your actor to use his upstage (away from the audience) arm. Otherwise he blocks part of his face and the dialogue may be lost.

Second, when playing space is limited, instruct your actors in the "hook" technique. (Illustration E) For example, if Mr. C is standing centerstage, he uses a hook to walk back to the table X. This keeps some angle of his face to the audience and makes the audience think you have a larger working space than you actually have. Also by walking in a small arc, he is now in a more open position to deliver his lines.

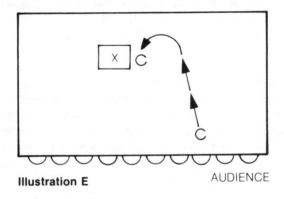

Illustration E   AUDIENCE

PERFORMING IN THE PULPIT AREA

In some churches, the sanctuary is the only available space and the pulpit cannot be moved. In that case, use the pulpit as a prop or if that is not possible, make it part of the set.

You might disguise it with banners, cover it with burlap, or set a black curtain drop in front of it. Most churches have flag-pole bases and they make effective banner holders. Get dowel screw sockets at any hardware store, take them apart and make them any length or height.

A screen in front of the pulpit (floor level) makes an excellent spot for slide projection. If you show slides or films in conjunction with the action on stage, be sure that the projected images supplement, not dominate, the action. Slides can be especially useful when a choir is singing and there is no movement on stage.

BLOCKING CROWDS OF PEOPLE

Expand the basic blocking notes for your principals to a choir of forty. Go back and look at Illustration A. A choir can be marched in or out from the four aisles. Illustration B is versatile too. Once on the stage in either of these playing spaces, the choir can give a script new dimension.

When you begin blocking the show, experiment on paper with "dressing" the playing area with your actors. Then try it out. You are creating a picture—one that starts and moves and has an end. Think in terms of the picture the audience will see and keep it interesting.

On a traditional stage, make use of all stairs and ramps leading to the stage. If the stage is too small or the acoustics are bad, do not feel obligated to use it. Consider setting up theatre-in-the-round or a three-quarter playing area. Perhaps your production could be staged in several different areas—one to the right, one to the left and one in front of the audience.

If you are working with the pulpit area, here are some ideas. Put some of the chorus in the choir loft. Bring them out to mill around in the main playing area and give them specific characters to pantomime or encourage them to think up their own characters. Next have them sit or stand on the stairs and finally exit through the audience. (Illustration F)

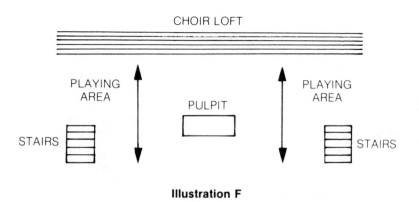

Illustration F

You can create the atmosphere of daily life in Judea, rush hour in Manhattan, or a lazy Sunday in suburbia, simply by changing the pace and quality of blocking.

Another idea (and one that makes choreography much easier) is to seat eight or ten choir members in chairs upstage and have them do motions with their hands and feet a la minstrel shows of yesteryear. If you use gloves, be sure they show up against the background. Another effect is to string people together to imitate the different parts of a machine. Use sounds as well as body movement to create the illusion.

FOCUS

Now that you have some ideas about blocking your choir, let's talk about your main actors or principals. Keep your choir several feet from your main characters so it is clear they are not part of the larger group. Use lighting and/or costumes to set them apart. If a principal has an entrance, bring him on downstage left or right or through the crowd. (Illustration G) or upstage center. (Illustration H).

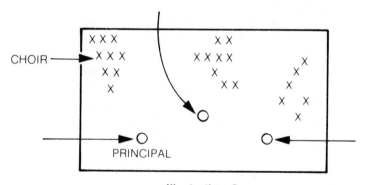

Illustration G

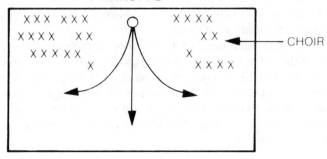

Illustration H

Generally speaking, downstage is a much stronger position for focus than upstage, except in formations like Illustration H. Different levels are also useful for focus. An actor who jumps on a box to deliver a speech receives immediate focus. A ladder will also give focus.

AUDIENCE PARTICIPATION

Audience participation is important because it sends people home feeling as if they were a part of what happened—and that's nice. The cast can walk in or out singing, greet the people, give them something, shower them with confetti, ask them to clap or sing along and they will think it's great. If audience participation is not in the script, use your imagination and add it in somewhere— even if the members of the cast just end their curtain calls by saying ''Goodnight.''

8.

SET DESIGN

The most effective set designs can also be the simplest and most economical. Abstract sets give you more flexibility than traditional three-sided box sets. Ordinary objects used with imagination make excellent sets. Banners, ladders, hat racks, stools, sawhorses, oversized picture frames, posters, cutouts, silhouettes, slides and films, even something as ordinary as a piece of rope can become a set.

Modular designs, geometric units of different heights, sizes and colors are also good examples of abstract sets.

HOW TO USE THE ABSTRACT

Here are a few effects you can create with an ordinary object, such as a ladder. Have an actor stand on it and it becomes a mountain, or a second story window, or a tree. Have him stand under it and it becomes a building, a doorway, a room, or perhaps the inner spaces of the mind.

Furniture groupings can indicate room or household divisions, eliminating the need for actual flats.

One of the most useful abstract designs is the cube. (If your group tours, do not overlook the dual function of your packing cases. Painted bright colors, they make ideal sets.)

Eight or ten cubes, which can be arranged in different ways, are a much better investment than risers, which restrict your movements and creativity.

Just to get you started, with eight cubes you can build a park, school room or a living room.

PARK LAYOUT NO. 1

PARK LAYOUT NO. 2

A SCHOOL ROOM

LIVING ROOM LAYOUT NO. 1

LIVING ROOM LAYOUT NO. 2

You can also vary the illusions created by the modular sets by draping or covering them with different materials. Make removable covers of calico, heavy-duty foil, denim or velvet.

Modular sets eliminate the need for stagehands. Actors can move the cubes themselves. Be sure to mark positions of the units on the stage floor with masking tape so the sets will go in the same place every time.

A construction note: put casters on the modular units so they can be easily moved. You can even work out simple choreography with these movable sets. Rubber swivel casters are the quietest.

BACKGROUND SETS

Slides are one of the most interesting backgrounds. You'll add a dimension to your production if you produce your own slides and/or films as a group project.

Colors set moods, red for excitement or intense emotion; green or blue for calm, pastoral feelings. If you have access to an overhead projector, a shallow dish containing oil, water and food coloring will produce interesting, changing color patterns.

Another interesting background is a black curtain drop or "black leg." White costumes—including tennis shoes—if washed in Tide will glow in the dark under a black light. Buy the flourescent tube black light that is sold in most poster stores. Use ultra-violet color filters for your spotlights. Buy these at any theatrical supply store.

If you have a front curtain, try projecting your slides on it. Have your actors stand in front of the curtains and relate to the projection. There will be shadows, but the abstract effect works very well.

Another idea is to cut a city skyline out of newspapers and pin it to the curtains. Or make white snowflakes or a crepe paper forest. Carry the theme through by covering the modular units with the same design.

If you are performing in the pulpit area, consider sets that hang from the ceiling. They take less space than standing flats. However if the ceiling is especially high, frames made of 1 × 2's with side wedges and covered with unbleached muslin make great backgrounds. Use them to mount banners, posters, cutouts, or even as multiple screens for slides and/or films.

In conclusion, the best set construction is what works for you. Don't overlook the simplest designs as they are often the most effective.

I also want you to meet Gilda Gant. Gilda teaches at Lamar University, Beaumont, Texas. Her masters degree in Fine Arts from the University of Oklahoma has been put to practical use in teaching writing, choreographing and performing. She has written a work called *Dance in the Christian Religion Today;* has choreographed such musicals as Godspell, My Fair Lady and Carousel; and has performed in numerous musicals staged in Casa Manana in Texas and the Country Dinner Playhouse in Dallas, Texas and Denver, Colorado. In addition to her university courses, Gilda also directs the jazz dance company and choreographs the University musicals.

9.

CHOREOGRAPHY

You do not have to be a dancer to set exciting, interesting movement. There are a few choreographic principles that are helpful when setting movement or dance on one performer or many. Not all have to move. You can choose one, two, four, or six. The others can be left in interesting freezes that can remain or be changed throughout the piece, they can exit, or they can be used as a movement chorus. The movement chorus functions much like the classic Greek chorus assuming postures or doing unison simple movements that suggest the mood of the piece being performed.

Since the chorus does not require much movement space, they can be placed off to one side or on a platform or series of cubes leaving the main area for the principal dancers. Listed below are several choreographic principles to consider when setting a movement piece.

FOCUS

Eye focus and the direction the body is facing make a statement about what is happening on stage. If one character needs to be the focal point at a particular time in the piece, placing that person facing the audience while the other performers face various angles to the sides and back will accomplish the needed focus. If all the dancers are facing front except one, the one that is different will receive the focus. When people are moving in the space and are not required to sing or speak, there is no reason that they cannot at times during the piece have their backs to the audience. A person facing the back of the performing area can be used as a strong statement within the piece and because we are three dimensional in our shape, it is nice to sometimes see more than the front of the body.

LEVEL

Utilizing levels always makes a dance or movement piece visually more interesting. This can be accomplished by varying the level of the dancers themselves or using platforms, cubes, stairs, etc. to vary the surface of the performing area. You can also vary

the levels of the dancers by choreographing in leaps, falls, knee work or floor work. It is usually impressive to see a group move in perfect unison and the steps can be very simple. It is exciting to see a group all fall to the floor together or leap in the air but to vary the piece, unison movement should be mixed with non-unison.

TIMING

When choreographing movement to a piece of music, the expected would be to fill each count with a movement. For example, a four count measure would have four movements. Varying the timing unexpectedly can lend an element of surprise. You can set several measures of one movement with each count, then suddenly double time the count doing two movements to one count, then switching back to one movement per count. You can also vary the timing by holding counts, going into slow motion or syncopation where you may move before or after the beat.

You may want to use several of these techniques in one piece. The majority of performers may be doing a set pattern of movement while a few others are varying the pattern using double time, freezes, or syncopation. The music often will suggest this kind of variation, for you can hear one or more musicians setting a different pattern *or* improvising over the basic sound and beat.

Whether the music suggests such a variation or simply stays with the same sound does not have to dictate what the choreographer chooses to do. It is also very interesting to work out movement with no music. The music does set the mood or nature of the piece. Without music the piece can go any direction and can change timing and mood at will. This can be more difficult for the choreographer, for without the music he or she has more decisions to make about what the mood or nature of the piece is going to be.

If you have not worked in silence before, it would be a good idea to do a short section without music and mix this with sections with music. You can also explore the possibilities of your performers making their own "music" by producing sounds with their hands, feet, bodies, or voices. It is really great fun to discover different sounds that you can make and then find movements that complement the sounds. You can approach it from the opposite direction by doing a movement and then deciding what sound it provokes. It is not necessary to have a sound for every movement.

DYNAMICS

Movement can be strong or weak, sudden or deliberate, heavy or light, fast or slow, loud or silent, or any number of combinations. Changing the dynamics of a piece gives it an element of the unexpected and allows the choreographer to change the direction of the mood or feeling of the dance. For example, if a group of dancers is moving easily together across the space and one dancer suddenly stops and strikes out with one fist, then continues with the others or goes in the opposite direction, the audience gets a feeling of reluctance or outright rebellion in that one dynamic alteration of the movement pattern. Experiment with similar movements.

MOTIVATION

Movement or dance can have a number of reasons for existence in a production. It can be used to help tell a story or explain a situation. For example, we see one move to another and cradle and rock that dancer. This visual statement of carryout is much stronger than just saying, "I am sorry about what happened." Putting in the rhythmical walking and rocking is in itself more comforting. So movement in a production can give the story more power and meaning.

However, dance does not have to tell a story or suggest a situation. It can be used to fill space in interesting ways or as a visual experience of any nature much like modern or abstract art. Dance patterns can be staged to constantly change like a kaleidoscope with lighting added to fade in and out and lend its magic.

SPACE

The use of the available space is very important. If there are set pieces, platforms, cubes, or props on stage, then the movement should use these things and not merely dance around them. Take advantage of the levels and props and gear the choreography to blend with, not oppose, the surroundings. If the stage is traditional, thrust, or in-the-round, look at the available space, entrances, exits, and plan the use of the space with imagination and variety.

Dancers do not have to start and stop a dance in the stage center area. The dance can start before the lights are up so it is in full swing when seen by the audience. The dancers can start off stage moving into the space and enter and exit throughout the piece. Beginning a dance that is part of a musical or story situation should be handled much like beginning a song. The music starts under the dialogue or song and the dance builds out of the situation.

When setting a dance movement pattern, consider whether it will be seen from above or below the performing area or both. Set the movement pattern so that it is exciting from many angles. It is a good idea to back off from the piece and look at it from the audiences' point of view. The dancers can start sitting in the audience and suddenly go in mass into the aisles and to the playing area. This can also be done one by one or in small groups. It is an enjoyable way of pulling the audience into the spirit of the production. You may also want to ask the audience to clap, sway, or stand up and shout to make them an active part of the performance. Whether you want actual audience participation depends on what kind of production you are doing.

COSTUMING THE DANCERS

It is often helpful to use costuming or props as part of the choreography. Hats, canes, and umbrellas can be used and are great fun. Capes and full skirts can add to the visual impact of a piece. A cape can be slipped off and used to imitate a bull fighter, or represent a body dropped to the earth, or a bird in flight, etc. Movement of the skirt can indicate the personality of the dancer. Flouncing movements could indicate anger or flirtation and nervous fingering and wadding convey shyness or sorrow. The use of scarves or bits of fabric is a good mood setter and often helps answer the question of what to do with the performer's hands.

The construction of costumes must be geared for movement. The fabric needs to have some elasticity and should fit loosely. If the costume is fitted, then the fabric needs a lot of give and gussets should be used under the arms. Costumes built off of a leotard allow you a good movement base. The main thing to remember is to inform the costumer before the patterns and fabric are bought, or costumes are rented, of what the various characters or dancers will be required to do physically.

Remember that dance steps and patterns do not have to be complicated to be exciting. You can take simple walking to music, add some levels, vary the timing of the walks, use interesting costumes and music, change the focus and dynamics and come up with a visually exciting movement piece. Experiment with different movements and see which best serves your purposes. Most of all, enjoy it!

DANCE IN CHURCH

A dance processional down the aisles to the front of the sanctuary is an effective way to start a sacred dance. Use stairs as level changes. You can build a platform stage in the choir loft, or front, or to one side. It depends on the breaking up of the space in a particular church. The advantage of a stage situation is spatial and visual. Your choreography is limited by the space available. The space in front of the church is not usually constructed with movement in mind, so if a stage is not built, then the audience will not be able to see any movement from the knees down. The choreography therefore should not be composed of intricate footwork, lower level movement like kneeling, or floorwork. Sit in several different areas, check the sight lines before choreographing and decide just what can be seen.

Movement can be set on one or many dancers depending on the space, what you wish to say with the dance, and the people available to participate. A dance can be set to a solo, duet, or entire choir and the singer can be located in the loft or balcony, congregation, or other available space. A soloist can sing from the pulpit while the dancer or dancers move to one side. You can use live musicians, a tape or record, or dance in silence.

One of the most effective experiences with religious dance can be movement expressing the spoken word. The minister may read a scripture, the priest intone a chant, or a children's choir tell a bible story with dancers expanding the meaning of the words through movement.

10.

CURTAIN CALLS

Curtain calls are very important because they give your cast a chance to receive the recognition they deserve. Don't leave them to chance. Block and rehearse them just as you would any other action on stage.

Here are some general principles.

Have the chorus enter from opposite sides of the stage, line up across the front and bow. If the chorus is large, make as many entrances as necessary. The point is to let everyone be seen. After the chorus has taken its bows, it should step back for the speaking performers to enter.

Group these actors according to the importance or duration of their roles, keeping the most important until last.

Each actor or group of actors enter, bow and step back for the next group. Alternating sides of the stage will add some visual interest.

When the entire cast is on stage, have everyone take a final bow and then exit in reverse order.

I would like you to know a fellow writer, John F. Wilson. John has composed a number of musicals for schools and churches including LET GEORGE DO IT, I BELIEVE, THE SMALL ONE, THE ELECTRIC SUNSHINE MAN and ENTERTAINMENT NOW AND THEN. As Executive Editor of Hope Publishing Company, as well as director of their Recording Division, John knows the music business as a composer, editor, producer and director. He also has had years of experience teaching and conducting choral groups in colleges, conventions and churches, having served as director of the Marion College Choir and Community Chorus, the Moody Men's Glee Club and presently the West Suburban Hospital Student Nurses' Choir, as well as his own recording group, The John Wilson Singers.

11.

TAPE TRACKS

An exciting new feature in the production of musicals today is the use of orchestral accompaniment tracks. If you have not performed with tape tracks yet, you and your singers are in for a unique experience.

Consider the advantages of employing (by way of tape tracks) the London Symphony Orchestra or the Los Angeles Strings to accompany your next musical. Very few schools, theatre groups or churches can afford to hire instrumentalists that could match these professional performers. Even if they could, the instrumentalists would be unable to fully recapture the "special effects" created in the recording studio by sophisticated mixing techniques, instrumental overdubbing, use of reverberation, intricately programmed electronic synthesizers and other tricks of the trade. Consider also the improved quality of performance your singers will give you. Good taped accompaniments set a musical standard that will bring the best out of your vocal group. The simple fact that the "tape goes on" forces them to be more rhythmic, to improve their attacks, releases and phrases. A well-tuned orchestral sound will also stimulate them to improve their pitch and intonation. The range and variety of instrumental sounds will help them "stylize" their singing more appropriately.

An increasing number of musicals are being produced with fully orchestrated demonstration recordings from which the tape tracks are made. This chapter will provide you with helpful hints on how to use them effectively.

WHAT TO LOOK FOR IN SELECTING TAPES

Before purchasing a tape, be sure you give it a good audition.

1) Judge the overall effectiveness of the instrumentation. If it includes a full orchestra and/or an exciting technological dimension of sound, the tape should be well worth your investment.

2) Determine whether or not you would feel comfortable with the conductor's tempi and dynamics and whether the quality of the tape reproduction is good.

It is generally agreed that monaural reproductions are more practical than stereophonic, because they give a better balance of sound throughout the auditorium.

CONDUCTING THE SINGERS

It has already been suggested that, when using a tape track, the role of the conductor is quite different. The conductor now becomes co-ordinator between the singers and the tape. In some ways this makes your job easier, since the tempi, dynamics and styles are already pre-determined, giving you more freedom to concentrate on phrasing, expression, diction and tone quality, and to become more "emotionally involved" with the drama and message content. It also means that the singers are at greater liberty to perform without a conductor, thus giving them more freedom to move about the stage or performing area. There are, however, several unique problems which must be solved, if you are to be in total command of the performance. Here are some suggestions for preparing both singers and conductors.

STEPS IN PREPARING TO USE TRACKS

1) Practice conducting the track several times prior to meeting with the singers, carefully notating any changes of tempi and dynamics in your score.

2) Count out the beat-lengths of each fermata, writing the number of beats above the notes being held. For example, a whole note which is normally 4 beats might be held for 7 or 8 beats. If you know this in advance, it will help you match your attacks and releases to the track.

3) Identify the rhythmic instruments. Perhaps the most difficult problem is "feeling" the beat, especially in the less rhythmic passages. Therefore, it is important to determine what instrument most clearly establishes the basic beat. Quite often it is the electric bass or the drum, but this is not always the case.

4) Identify "cues." Often it is difficult to count measures and beat time throughout musical interludes and narrations, so most orchestral arrangers have provided musical "cues" to indicate vocal entries. Often it is a chime, a glissando, a drum or cymbal or a short melodic line in a solo instrument. The director and singers can use these to establish beats and pitches.

5) If the tape does not run continuously through the performance, you may want to pre-time the length of "leader tape" between each selection, or perhaps re-edit the tape to give you the exact amount of leader you need for each entry. Tape starting cues should be marked in both the conductor's and the engineer's scores.

EQUIPMENT NEEDED

In addition to the microphones, speakers and amplifiers discussed in the forthcoming chapters, you will need a *tape deck* which can be connected to your mixer unit. You will probably also need one or more *monitors*, especially if the auditorium speakers are located some distance from your singers.

TAPE DECKS
Before purchasing a tape deck, you must decide whether you want to use *reel-to-reel* tapes or *cassettes*. Here are several factors, all of which should be considered before making this decision.

1) Quality of reproduction. Most musicians agree that reel-to-reel tapes produce a higher quality of sound than cassettes. This is especially noticeable on the high and low partials of voices and

instruments. However, manufacturers are now producing 2 speed cassette decks which play at both 1⅞ IPS (the present normal speed) and 3¾ IPS, which gives a much improved quality of sound.

2) Availability. Nearly all accompaniment tracks are available in 7½ IPS reel-to-reel tapes. However, an increasing number of 1⅞ IPS cassettes are now being manufactured, and some companies offer both. There are legal restrictions prohibiting you from reproducing your own cassettes from the available reel-to-reel tapes (or vice versa).

3) Ease of handling. The cassette deck and the cassettes are both smaller and easier to handle than their reel-to-reel counterparts. There are also fewer exposed parts which can be damaged in transporting. In addition to this the cassettes are easier to rewind and reload in the deck. For these reasons, many travelling groups favor cassettes. To many performers, the degree of difference in quality between the two is not as important an issue as the convenience, the ease of handling and the set up time.

Recommended Tape Decks.* The following recommendations are classified according to price range.

Reel to Reel 7½ IPS
High	TEAC	2300
Medium	Akai	GX—230D**
Low	Akai	1722

Cassette 1⅞ IPS
High	Akai	GXC—750 D
Medium	Akai	GXC—709 D
Low	Akai	CS—702 D

2 Speed Cassette 1⅞ and 3¾ IPS
BIC	T-4
BIC	T-3
BIC	T-2
BIC	T-1

---

*With thanks to Howard Parker, author of the chapters on equipment, for his specific recommendations.

**D indicates Dolby noise reduction system.

MONITORS

Any reasonably good speaker may be used as a monitor, as long as it reproduces a clear sound and is not so large as to get in the way of, or distract from, the stage activity. It must, however, be amplified separately so that it carries the orchestra tracks only, and not the "live" performers' voices.

LOCATION OF SPEAKERS AND MONITORS

The positioning of speakers and monitors will vary according to the size of the auditorium, the stage area and the amount of movement which will take place during the performance. The following positions should be considered.

Position 1. One speaker, located behind and elevated above the heads of the singers. This may be all that is necessary for a small group in a rather small stage area or choir loft. The major problem you will confront is that of "feedback" which may occur if the microphones are within the sound pattern of the speaker.

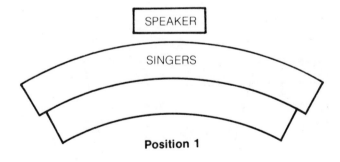

Position 1

Position 2. Two speakers, located behind and elevated above the singers, angled slightly so that the sound patterns cross at about the halfway point in the auditorium listening area. This is especially effective in a long, but narrow room. Again, you must be careful that feedback doesn't occur (as in Position 1).

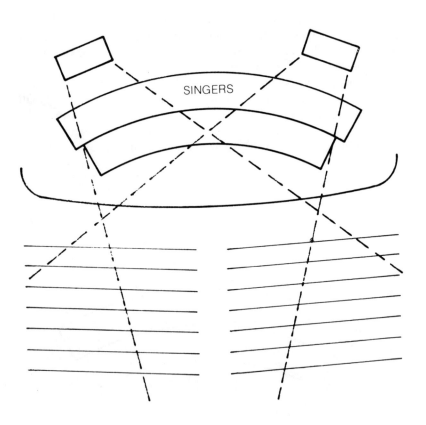

Position 3. Two (or more) speakers located on either side and possibly elevated above the singers' heads with one monitor in front and facing the singers. For proper distribution of sound in a large or wide auditorium, it is often necessary to place the speakers some distance away from the singers, thus making it difficult for them to hear the tracks. This is when the use of a monitor is important.

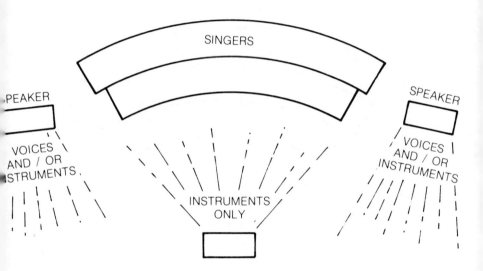

OTHER MONITOR POSITIONS

It is important that monitors be properly placed so that all singers and actors (who need to) can hear the accompaniment tracks equally well at all times. If this is difficult to accomplish with the above suggestion, the following alternate positions ought to be considered.

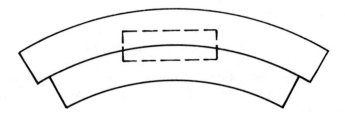

Below risers, projecting up

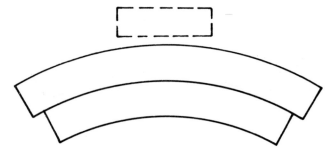

Behind singers (but not above)
projecting into singers

All of the above positions are designed to accommodate the stationary singing group on a small to moderately large stage. If you have a large stage and/or the activity is spread out over a wide area, it may be necessary to have monitors placed in more than one location, in front or on either side of the singers (or both). See illustrations.

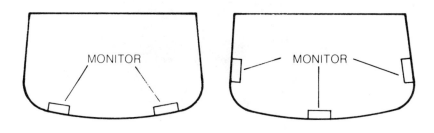

Since the stage areas in schools and churches differ greatly, these suggestions may be merely the first steps toward some very creative, unique experimentation you must conduct to find the ideal setup for your own particular needs. It is important to remember that any use of overhead or lapel mikes will add to the dangers of feedback and must be checked out carefully. Any use of curtains will also increase your problems in finding ideal positions for speakers and monitors, especially if some of the activities take place in front of closed curtains and others on an open stage.

IN SUMMARY

There are arguments, both pro and con, regarding the use of taped accompaniments. In many instances the tapes will add a very exciting new dimension to your program. In some cases you may choose to use "live" instrumentalists. In fact, there may even be times when you will choose to use both on the same program. By all means, let your choir enjoy the experience of using tapes. However, before you do, be sure you have 1. the proper equipment to make it a pleasurable experience, and 2. sufficient time to rehearse with the tapes to make your performance as trouble-free and as professional sounding as possible.

Finally let me present Howard Parker, a sound systems specialist and President of Sound Investment Enterprises. He has designed and supplied systems for Ralph Carmichael, the Hawaiians, Continental Singers, Dino, Jeremiah People, New Hope, Renaissance, New Life Singers, Act One Co., and Campus Crusade. Howard also does workshops for major publishing and recording companies. He is currently traveling throughout the United States and Canada teaching audio seminars for church people entitled Sound Shop.

12.

SOUND SYSTEMS

Having good quality components that are within your financial reach is a necessity. The quality determines the naturalness of the sound and controls the amount of feedback you encounter. Outward appearances will tell you very little about how well components work.

Every professional sound-system designer has specific guidelines that he has learned over the years. They are not black magic. They can be applied by anyone. Follow these guidelines, because they are as basic as the law of gravity.

MICROPHONES

Low impedance and unidirectional microphones will allow you the longest cable lengths and the greatest feedback control.

Low impedance (low Z) microphones have a number rating anywhere from 75 to 600 ohms. Low Z permits you to have microphone cables up to 1000 feet without any change in quality. High impedance microphones are limited to a maximum cable length of 18 feet between the microphone and the mixer input.

FEEDBACK

Simply defined, feedback is amplified sound that has come from the speakers and re-entered the microphone. A microphone that rejects sound from the audience direction will have a lower potential to feedback. Unidirectional (Cardioid) microphones pick up the greatest volume of sound from straight on or the "on axis" position. As you move to the sides, the volume drops off. This rejection of sound on the sides and back of the unidirectional microphone helps minimize feedback.

GENERAL RECOMMENDATIONS

A Dynamic microphone is high quality and extremely rugged. It is not as sensitive to temperature, mishandling or moisture as a condenser or ribbon microphone. It is, therefore, ideal in most general miking applications.

A Condenser microphone is higher quality, but it is very delicate. The condenser microphone requires a power supply to operate. Some condensers take a battery inside their case while others require that the power supply be external, either somewhere along the microphone line or built into the mixer. Condensers should only be used in situations where they can be protected from rough handling and abuse. Ribbon microphones are very fragile and are only recommended for special applications.

13.

MICROPHONE RECOMMENDATIONS

The microphones that work best in most applications are:

Hand Held Solo
   First choice   Shure SM-58CN
   Second choice   Electro Voice 1776 or 1777
   Third choice   AKG D330BT

The solo microphone should always be held slightly below the mouth at approximately chin level. Do not let the microphone cover or block the mouth from the audience.

The colored windscreens by Shure Bros. (model A61WS, available in 9 colors) are ideal for minimizing popping sounds caused by P's and T's. They are also a great help to the technician in telling which microphones are where.

Small Groups
   First choice   Neumann KM-84
   Second choice   Shure SM-58CN

Always select a unidirectional microphone to help control feedback. Place the vocalists at varying distances from the microphone. The person singing directly into the mike should be farthest away and those on the sides should be closer (a horseshoe formation). This gives equal volume pickup of each voice.

Choir

First choice   Neumann KM-84
Second choice   AKG C451E
Third choice   Shure SM-81

To keep the microphones as invisible as possible, hang them overhead. Hang them one foot in front of and two to three feet above the heads of the front choir row and point them at the back row. Microphone cable is now available in ten different colors so you can select a color that blends with your decor.

Speaker's Stand

First choice   Neumann KM-84
Second choice   AKG C451E
Third choice   Shure SM-81

Mount the microphones as close to the person speaking or singing as possible. This insures the highest quality sound and the least chance of feedback. Usually a gooseneck, available in 6, 13, or 19 inch lengths, is the easiest way to mount the podium microphone.

Stage Microphones

First choice   AKG C451E with the Ck-8 shotgun capsule
Second choice   Electro-Voice DL-42
Third choice   Sennheiser MKE 802

Shotgun microphones are used for dramatic sound pickup. Place them over the stage or near the stage floor and point them to specific areas where you need sound pickup. Do not attempt to make the whole stage "hot" with microphones. Decide exactly what areas can be successfully miked and work your drama into them.

14.

MIXERS

There are several rules that must be followed when considering and operating mixers:

Mixer input impedances must match the microphones. Since low impedance microphones will give you the greatest cable length, you should also have low impedance inputs on your mixer. However, it is possible to mix high impedance and low impedance if you use a line matching transformer. Shure Bros. make some excellent ones.

When connecting a low impedance microphone to a high impedance mixer input, you need a model A95UF.

When connecting a high impedance microphone to a low impedance mixer input, you need a model A95U.

Remember the A95U must not be more than 18 feet from the high impedance microphone.

Tape recorder outputs must be matched to the mixer input. Since a tape output signal is "line" or "auxiliary level," the input on the mixer must be able to handle that form of signal and impedance. If the mixer has only low impedance microphone inputs, then a Shure line matching transformer, model A97A, is necessary to convert the tape output to a low impedance microphone type signal.

If the mixer has high impedance microphone inputs, then a Switchcraft mini-mixer, model 311, should be placed just before the mixer input to protect against distortion.

CHECKLIST

Here is a quick checklist of do's and don't's concerning mixers.
1) The mixer or console should be located in the audience so the technician can mix based upon what the audience hears.
2) Tone controls should not be run at extreme positions.
3) Reverberation should be used to compliment the sound, but not so much that it draws attention to itself.
4) Feedback filters should not be used unless absolutely necessary
5) The sound technician should use his ears, not the VU meters, to set levels and make adjustments. VU meters are for broadcast and recording, not live performances.

MIXER RECOMMENDATIONS

UNI-SYNC Trouper I
    8 inputs with reverb and monitor send

DMI Kelsey 8 + 1 Pro Club
    8 inputs plus effects send

15.

AMPLIFIERS AND SPEAKERS

These components are so important to your program and overall sound, yet they are often improperly matched. You must know the requirements of the speakers BEFORE you can decide on the amplifier. Here are some critical rules for proper selection and use of amplifiers and speakers.

Amplifier power output ratings must match the power requirements of all speakers connected.

An amplifier is like an engine in a car. It takes a larger engine to power a heavier automobile. The more inefficient the speaker, the more power it takes to reach the same listening volume. Two 50-watt speakers will need to be powered by a 100-watt (or slightly higher) amplifier. You always add the wattage ratings of all speakers together to find the power output needed by your amplifier.

Speaker impedance or the combination of speaker impedances must be matched properly to the amplifier.

Two speakers rated at 16 ohms each will cause the amplifier to see an 8-ohm load. Three 16-ohm speakers will appear to the amplifier as 5.3 ohms. Two 8-ohm speakers create a 4-ohm load on the amplifier. The importance of all this is that the wattage output from the amplifier is changed by the impedance load it sees.

An amplifier that puts out 50 watts into a 16-ohm load may deliver 100 watts into an 8-ohm load, based upon its design and ratings.

Therefore, the output power of the amplifier must be coordinated with the combined impedance of all speakers connected. An improper impedance match can result in severe damage to the amplifier and to the speakers. Check your speaker and amplifier specification sheets for proper power and impedance requirements or call a dealer for assistance.

GENERAL RULES

Speakers should be placed so the audience is looking and hearing in the same direction.

We automatically turn toward the source of a sound. Therefore, a good rule of thumb when placing the speakers is to have them in line with the microphones, or on the audience side, and place them one-third of the way in from each side wall. This keeps them close enough to the center for natural sound and far enough away from the side walls to minimize sound reflections. Point the speakers toward the center of the back row, or toward the back of the center aisle.

Speakers must be seen to be heard.

Place all speakers far enough over the heads of the audience so that everyone can see them. Sound travels in straight lines, like light from a flashlight. If a person can't see the speakers, he can't hear them. He hears only indirect or reflected sound. Tilt speakers down toward the audience.

SYSTEM RECOMMENDATIONS

1) SHURE 700 Console with 6 mic. inputs, 2 tape inputs, reverb, 2 200 watt amplifiers ....47 lbs.
   SHURE 701 Speakers with 15" bass speaker and high frequency horn ....58 lbs. each

2) BOSE PM-2 Console with 6 mic. inputs, 1 tape input, reverb, and 400 watt amplifier ....70 lbs.
   BOSE 802 (1 pair) speakers including travel lid .35 lbs. each

3) AUDIO LOGIC Model 180 SA 18 input mixer, stereo output, reverb, 18 VU meters, 2 155 watt amplifiers ....90 lbs.
COMMUNITY PBL speakers with high quality JBL components ....75 lbs. each

Each of the above complete mixer/amplifier/speaker systems is compatible with the recommended microphones and would be ideal for either portable or permanent installation use.

16.

CABLES

Cables are another area that need some attention. They can be the flaw in an otherwise beautiful system. Here are some guidelines for choosing and maintaining cables.

All cables, before and up to the amplifier, must be shielded.

Shielding protects the yet unamplified signal from outside interferences. The shield is the braded wire or tin foil that is just inside the rubber or vinyl jacket of the cable.

Any cable without the shield will allow problems no matter how short the cable is. Shielding is not necessary for speaker cables.

All speaker cables must be large enough in gauge (wire diameter) to accommodate the amplified signal.

An amplifier may only produce one half or less of its rated output power if the speaker cable is too small in diameter. Two factors that determine cable gauge are impedance load of all speakers on that cable and the length of the cable from the amplifier to the last speaker. The following chart shows proper gauge of cable based on distance and impedance load.

Wire Gauge	4 ohms	8 ohms	16 ohms
10	240'	480'	960'
12	150'	300'	600'
14	96'	192'	380'
16	60'	120'	240'
18	38'	76'	152'
20	24'	48'	96'
22	14'	28'	56'

These are the maximum speaker cable lengths (in feet) for no more than 10% amplifier power loss.

Use stranded conductor cable for portable, and solid conductor cable for permanent applications.

The stranded conductor cable allows the flexing needed for portable applications. For permanent installations, the solid conductor cable is acceptable and the cost is slightly less. For portable speaker cables, use a high quality electrical cord with two conductors, each conductor coded with a separate color. For installations use TW type electrical wire, giving each conductor a separate color.

All microphone and speaker cables must be in polarity with each other or sound quality and audience coverage will suffer.

When checking three-pin cannon-type microphone cables, be sure that the shield is always connected to pin one on each end. The white or lighter conductor should be connected to pin two and the black or darker conductor should be soldered onto pin three. With speaker cables, the white or lighter conductor should always be connected to the tip of the ¼ inch phone plug and the black or darker conductor should be connected to the sleeve or ground.

An excellent tool to check this periodically is the Sound Investment cable tester model PS-74. This tester also checks for shorts and broken lines.

SOUND SUMMARY

In summary let me point out that even after weeks of rehearsal, preparation, and planning, your program will only be as good as the sound system and its operator. The finest components, if not properly matched or interconnected, cannot do their best job. A technician with a strong desire to help, but without proper background or training, can do much to teach you patience but will not enhance your program.

When in doubt about sound, look to a professional for advice and help. Often the advice is free and whatever his fee is for help, it will be better than the hours and days of frustration. Help your technician attend a training class or two on sound systems. Both he and you will be the better for it.

SUPPLIERS

COSTUMES & MAKEUP

Atlanta Costume
2089 Monroe Dr. NE
Atlanta, GA 30324
404-874-7511

Texas Costume
2125 North Harwood St.
Dallas, TX 75201
214-748-4581

SOUND EQUIPMENT

Sound Investment Enterprises
P.O. Box 4139
Thousand Oaks, CA 91359
213-991-3400

Sound Investment Enterprises
P.O. Box 14825
Austin, TX 78761
512-837-4646

LIGHTING EQUIPMENT

Norcostco
2089 Monroe Dr. NE
Atlanta, GA 30324
404-874-7511

AUDIO SEMINARS/CONSULTATION

Sound Investment Enterprises
P.O. Box 14825
Austin, TX 78761
512-837-4646

INDEX